THIS BOOK BELONGS TO

Calm

_____

Copyright © 2022 Amary Education LLC

First Edition: August 2022

Sign up for updates, and book companion activity giveaways at www.amaryacademy.com. Stay tune for updates and new releases on Instagram and Facebook @amaryacademy
ISBN 9798833676912 (Paperback)

Please email bulk order requests to info@amaryeducation.com.

www.amaryacademy.com

ADVENTURES OF AMARY
Becoming Calm

KHRYSANTA MAREI

I see red when I am mad.
Sometimes I can't help how I feel.
Anger is an emotion that I can't hide.

Expressing my emotion is okay, but
I do and say things I don't mean.
I regret it because it is not me.

I get mad when I have to share my toys.

I get mad when I am frustrated and can't do the things I want to do.

This is Happy, my positive cloud.
He reminds me to calm down when I get mad.

But there are times when I can't control
how I feel...

...I get mad because I feel that something it is unfair or not right. When I am angry, I feel strong.
My anger keeps me safe and away from getting hurt.

But the longer I feel this way,
the more I feel heavy and unhappy.

When I lose control of my anger, I hurt the people around me which makes them upset and sad.

My anger gets me into trouble: keeping me away from making friends, receiving love, or being happy.

When I feel angry,
my body feels hot, my tummy rumbles, my heart
pounds, and I sweat.
I hate how I feel and how my body feels.

I am in control, I need to stop and calm myself down.
I take five big deep breaths and I say:

This is not me!

I am Amary, I choose to feel good and to not hurt
other people's feelings.

Listen to Happy...

Take a rest, and it will get better when you wake up. I know you are upset, and it is okay.

It will go away. Our feelings come and go. You are in control and your emotions are valid.

Emotions come in different sizes. They come in big or small, but Happy came to remind me that it is okay to have feelings but we have the power to control how we act and react.

Being angry makes me tired. But choosing to use my energy to create positive moments makes me feel better and happier.

When I am mad,
I pause and take a big deep breath:
Breathing through my nose and releasing it
through my mouth.
I repeat this step 5 times or until my body feels
calm.

I tell myself positive words, and I write them down on a piece of paper to turn them into positive thoughts. I say things like...

When I am irritated, I take a
nap to feel better and
re-energize my body.

And when I am rested and feel better, I go out with my friends or family to play and have a good time.

When I hurt someone with my actions, I apologize, I say things like, "I am sorry. I overreacted because I was angry."

I learn how to calm myself, and acknowledge my mistake. I apologize for hurting the people I care about.

I need to release my emotions like anger or frustration, and I try my best to remind myself that my feelings do not define me and that I am beautiful on the inside.

My emotions of today don't define how I will feel tomorrow. It is not because I am angry today that tomorrow needs to be a bad day.

I have the power to wake up happy and spread love and happiness throughout the day.

Remember to always see the good in ourselves and other people.

We are the actor of our life, and we have the power to turn our anger into joy and happiness.
Life is too short to not embrace it fully by spreading love and happiness around us!

MORE THAN JUST A BOOK!

Introducing Amary SEL Web App.

Our web application offers fun and engaging games to learn more about themselves while developing important social and emotional skills. Through interactive games, activities, and quizzes, children can explore various emotions, learn how to express themselves effectively, and practice important life skills such as problem-solving and decision-making.

 4-12

 Social-emotional Learning Web App

 Ideal at-home activity for kids.

 Try our 7-day free trial. Fill up the form to receive the link.
www.amaryacademy.com/e-learning/

SCAN ME

Amary's Next Adventures:

Printed in Great Britain
by Amazon

22953999R10025